S0-CDP-325

A Healthy Body

Characteristics of a *Contagious* Church

Charles R. Swindoll

A Healthy Body
Characteristics of a Contagious Chu~
By Charles R. Swindoll

Charles R. Swindoll has devoted his life to the accurate, practical tea~ and application of God's Word and His grace. A pastor at heart, Chuc~ has served as senior pastor to congregations in Texas, Massachusetts, and California. Since 1998, he has served as the founder and senior pastor-teacher of Stonebriar Community Church in Frisco, Texas, but Chuck's listening audience extends far beyond a local church body. As a leading program in Christian broadcasting since 1979, *Insight for Living* airs in major Christian radio markets around the world, reaching people groups in languages they can understand. Chuck's extensive writing ministry has also served the body of Christ worldwide and his leadership as president and now chancellor of Dallas Theological Seminary has helped prepare and equip a new generation for ministry. Chuck and Cynthia, his partner in life and ministry, have four grown children, ten grandchildren, and two great-grandchildren.

Published By
IFL Publishing House
A Division of Insight for Living Ministries
Post Office Box 251007
Plano, Texas 75025-1007

Editor in Chief: Cynthia Swindoll, President, Insight for Living
Executive Vice President: Wayne Stiles, Th.M., D.Min., Dallas Theological Seminary
Editor: Malia E. Rodriguez, Th.M., Dallas Theological Seminary
Content Editor: Amy L. Snedaker, B.A., English, Rhodes College
Copy Editors: Jim Craft, M.A., English, Mississippi College
Kathryn Merritt, M.A., English, Hardin-Simmons University
Project Coordinator, Creative Ministries: Noelle Caple, M.A., Christian Education, Dallas Theological Seminary
Project Coordinator, Publishing: Melissa Cleghorn, B.A., University of North Texas
Proofreader: Paula McCoy, B.A., English, Texas A&M University-Commerce
Art Director: Mike Beitler, B.F.A., Graphic Design, Abilene Christian University
Designer: Laura Dubroc, B.F.A., Advertising Design, University of Louisiana at Lafayette
Production Artist: Nancy Gustine, B.F.A., Advertising Art, University of North Texas

Unless otherwise identified, Scripture quotations are from the *New American Standard Bible*® (NASB). Copyright © 1960, 1962, 1963, 1968, 1971, 1972, 1973, 1975, 1977, 1995 by The Lockman Foundation, La Habra, California. All rights reserved. Used by permission. (www.lockman.org)

An effort has been made to locate sources and obtain permission where necessary for the quotations used in this booklet. In the event of any unintentional omission, a modification will gladly be incorporated in future printings.

ISBN: 978-1-57972-976-9
Printed in the United States of America

A Healthy Body

Characteristics of a *Contagious* Church

Charles R. Swindoll

A Letter from Chuck

Are you looking for a church? On a search for just any church . . . or a truly healthy one? Or do you wonder if your church follows the biblical model?

If you live in some parts of the world, you may pass ten churches on your way to the supermarket. In others, you may spend an hour or more making your way to the nearest church on Sunday morning. Whether you live among an abundance of churches or just a few, I hope you have chosen one you call *your* church home. Maybe you're in the process of selecting one right now.

As you consider the church you serve in or a potential church, ask yourself, why it is that you wake up early on Sunday morning to go *there* specifically? Why do you invest your time, your talents, and your money there? Do you attend in order to sing your favorite Christian songs or hymns or to hear a dynamic pastor preach? Or do you go to learn God's Word, to pray with fellow believers, to give and receive grace, and, mainly, to worship God? In other words, do you know the characteristics of a healthy, Christ-centered congregation?

After more than five decades of pastoral ministry, I'm convinced that postmodernism has initiated a silent, subtle erosion in the church. Once steeped in theological wisdom and driven to display God's glory, many congregations have become derailed into providing entertainment and functioning in superficiality and futility. If a church isn't traveling in the right direction, it'll never reach its glorious destination. That's tragic—and the consequences are far-reaching.

Is your church on track, or has it been derailed? How do you know for sure? Whether you are a church leader or member, this booklet will help you spot the distinctive characteristics of a healthy church.

As you work your way through *A Healthy Body: Characteristics of a Contagious Church*, I hope the Lord will open your eyes to the purpose of the church. I also hope He will show you how your specific local congregation can act as a beacon of light in the midst of a darkening culture. I *urge* you to commit yourself to God's great work in the church. The church is, after all, the primary means God uses to grow His followers *in* Christ and to reach our culture *for* Christ. He can do this through us . . . if we remain fully committed and willing to submit ourselves to Him as Lord. It's a calling worth striving for.

Praying for renewal in the church,

Charles Swindoll

Charles R. Swindoll

A Healthy Body: Characteristics of a Contagious Church

I wish I could have been there to see it.

It was 7:51 a.m. on January 12, 2007. L'Enfant Plaza in Washington, D.C., a busy subway station, had its usual morning rush of commuters.

A young man wearing a baseball cap, T-shirt, and faded jeans entered the plaza and quietly removed his violin from its case. He tossed in some seed money to bait the passersby and lifted the violin to his chin. The player? Joshua Bell, possibly the finest violinist of our generation. His instrument? The rare Gibson ex Huberman, handcrafted in 1713 by Antonio Stradivari, one of the most coveted and expensive violins in existence. The music? Bell began with "Chaconne," from Bach's Partita No. 2 in D Minor, hailed by some as one of the greatest pieces of music ever composed. The response? You'd be surprised.

Of the 1,097 commuters who passed Bell that morning, only seven stopped to listen. That's right . . . *seven*. Just three days earlier, Bell had played to a sold-out crowd at Boston's Symphony Hall where the average seat cost $100. His earnings that morning in the subway? A little over $32. Bell usually earns around $1,000 a minute.[1] (I should have stayed with the violin!)

The Washington Post sponsored Bell's incognito performance in order to evaluate the public's taste, priorities, and perception. But for me, the experience remains a powerful lesson on the importance of something else.

Context.

No matter how beautifully Joshua Bell played his Stradivarius, and no matter how exquisite his musical selection may have been, it took more. His giftedness wasn't enough. It took a *context* that was conducive and favorable to it.

I find the same true of preaching.

Excellent exposition of the Scriptures alone isn't enough to cause people to continue attending and to stick together as a church. It takes more.

Please don't misunderstand. I'm certainly not diminishing the importance of preaching God's Word. I simply mean there are preachers all around the world who faithfully declare the truth . . . and yet their local church is not growing. In fact, I used to serve at such a church. I preached just as passionately there as I do in my current ministry. But there was no growth. The marks of an attractive church weren't present. In fact, I remember one Fourth of July weekend when there were seven people in the entire place . . . and four of them were Swindolls! That was *not* an inviting context. I might as well have been preaching in the subway.

Why is it we will drive past any number of churches in order to worship at one particular church located farther from our house than all the rest? What is it that draws us in, causing us to stay excited about, invest our time and money, and become an active participant of that church instead of some other? How can one ministry become so attractive, so meaningful to us, that we're willing to adjust our lives to fit its schedule, rear our children in it, and even invite other people to come with us?

The best word to describe such an attraction is *contagious*. Webster defined the root word, *contagion*, as "an influence that spreads rapidly." [2] When a church is in this category, word quickly travels. People witness the passion in our enthusiasm. They hear the excitement in our voices.

They see characteristics that set our church apart. They finally become so curious they come to see for themselves. One thing is for sure: they observe a set of distinctives being modeled like nothing the world around them has to offer. A contagious church is unique.

Some movies have quotes that have become so inimitable, so distinctive, that you could say the first part of the line, and most folks could finish it for you. Let's try a few:

"Houston, we have _____."

"Go ahead, make _____."

"Of all the gin joints in all the towns in all the world, she _____."

"Frankly, my dear, I don't . . ." (Well, let's not go there!)

The movie *Field of Dreams* has one of those lines as well: "If you build it" — can you finish the quote? — "he will come." Some people think it's "*they* will come." In fact, when I graduated from seminary, long before the movie came out, I thought a similar line would be true in the church: *if you preach it, they will come.* Wow! Was I wrong.

I have lived to realize that, while a strong pulpit is essential, a contagious church also requires a context of other essentials and distinctives. There must be more than preaching. More than one gift at work. More than the conviction of one person. A contagious church has a number of individuals living out clear, biblical principles with the result that people pause in the midst of their busy lives. They realize this is a place worth their coming and participating.

When you look across the landscape of churches today, you find many congregations that have experienced phenomenal growth. Unbelievable growth. But upon closer examination, you discover that they have not committed themselves to the four biblical essentials for a church as prescribed in the book of Acts.

Four Essentials for Every Church

In spite of the tremendous growth of the early church and all the demands of a group that large, there was still simplicity. There was no tradition; there were no church constitution and bylaws, no programs, no senior pastor, no "board of elders," no marketing plan, no splinter groups, no corruption—and no erosion . . . not yet. Instead, we see 3,120 people living their lives with the Spirit of God now living within them and directing their steps. So what did that look like? We're told precisely what those early believers did when they met together. Look closely:

> They were continually devoting themselves to the apostles' teaching and to fellowship, to the breaking of bread and to prayer. (Acts 2:42)

In this one verse we have the lowest common denominator of a church. This is ground zero. It would help greatly if God's people reminded themselves of this single verse of Scripture every day. When the first body of believers gathered together, they devoted themselves to four essentials. Did you notice them? Here are the four essentials: *teaching*, *fellowship*, *breaking of bread*, and *prayer*. The church may have more than these four . . . but it must not have less. This verse is not only *descriptive* of what the early church did; it is also *prescriptive* of what all churches must do.

For a church to be the kind of church Jesus promised to build, there must be *teaching*, which, of course, includes preaching. Teaching is not the same as mere talking, or reading poetry, or motivational speaking, or delivering a positive-thinking-type devotional. We are told here what type of teaching it means: they devoted themselves to the *apostles'* teaching. Today the

8

church has the apostles' teaching represented in the complete Word of God — the Bible. A church must continually be devoted to the teaching of the sacred Scriptures. Teaching God's truth gives a church deep roots that provide nourishment and stability.

For a church to be the kind of church Jesus promised to build, there has to be *fellowship* as well. If we had teaching without fellowship, the church would be a school — a place that simply dispenses information. The original term for fellowship is *koinonia*, which refers to close, mutual relationships where people share things in common and remain involved with one another. That doesn't mean potluck suppers, dinners on the grounds, and Christmas concerts.

Koinonia represents close relationships that involve sharing life with one another — the bad times as well as the good. Those in fellowship with one another cultivate an intimate harmony with others. In church, the Word of God is not only *learned* through teaching . . . it is *lived* through fellowship.

The *breaking of bread* is included along with teaching and fellowship. That refers to the Lord's Table, which was observed when the church gathered. Because baptism was mentioned just before this verse, we understand that the early church devoted itself to the two ordinances commanded by Jesus: baptism and the Lord's Table. The first represents our conversion to Christ, and the second, our lifelong communion with Him. An acceptable, all-inclusive term would be *worship*. For a church to be the kind of church Jesus promised to build, there must be worship.

Finally, they devoted themselves to *prayer*. They spent time as a body of believers adoring their Lord, confessing their sins, interceding for others, petitioning God to provide, and thanking Him for His blessings—just as Jesus taught them to pray. For a church to be the kind of church Jesus promised to build, there must be prayer.

You can't have a church if you take away any of the four essentials recorded in Acts 2:42. You can have *more* than these four, but you cannot have *less* and still be a church. And if you have more—and most churches do—those things added must never contradict or obscure the importance of the essentials. When they do, count on it, erosion occurs.

Remarkably, the simple setting of the original church provided room for the Spirit of God to work and guide. Don't misunderstand; a simple setting does not suggest perfect people. These new believers were far from flawless. But by the empowerment of the Spirit of God as He worked and controlled their lives, there was integrity, trust, joy, confidence, unity, generosity, forgiveness, compassion, harmony, stability, and, of course, grace (to name only a few). It must have been magnificent! Was it working? Just look at the verses that follow:

> Day by day continuing with one mind in the temple, and breaking bread from house to house, they were taking their meals together with gladness and sincerity of heart, praising God and having favor with all the people. And the Lord was adding to their number day by day those who were being saved. (Acts 2:46–47)

Read that again, and this time, observe the vertical as well as the horizontal. Also notice that, as a result of the believers' devoting themselves to the essentials, the church continued to expand and grow. Truth be told, the growth was off-the-chart remarkable—even in an era of persecution. Look at how the church continued to enlarge as the months and years unfolded:

But many of those who had heard the message believed; and the number of the men came to be about five thousand. (Acts 4:4)

And all the more believers in the Lord, multitudes of men and women, were constantly added to their number. (Acts 5:14)

The word of God kept on spreading; and the number of the disciples continued to increase greatly in Jerusalem, and a great many of the priests were becoming obedient to the faith. (Acts 6:7)

So the church throughout all Judea and Galilee and Samaria enjoyed peace, being built up; and going on in the fear of the Lord and in the comfort of the Holy Spirit, it continued to increase. (Acts 9:31)

And the hand of the Lord was with them, and a large number who believed turned to the Lord. The news about them reached the ears of the church at Jerusalem, and they sent Barnabas off to Antioch. Then when he arrived and witnessed the grace of God, he rejoiced and began to encourage them all with resolute heart to remain true to the Lord; for he was a good man, and full of the Holy Spirit and of faith. And considerable numbers were brought to the Lord. (Acts 11:21–24)

In Iconium they entered the synagogue of the Jews together, and spoke in such a manner that a large number of people believed, both of Jews and of Greeks. (Acts 14:1)

So the churches were being strengthened in the faith, and were increasing in number daily. (Acts 16:5)

Therefore many of them believed, along with a number of prominent Greek women and men. (Acts 17:12)

Again, the growth was remarkable! In spite of intense opposition and persecution—and sometimes *because of it*—Christ continued to build His church. Theologian and historian F. F. Bruce calls this phenomenon "the spreading flame."[3] The growth continued to crescendo, just as Jesus promised. And the adversary, as hard as he may have tried, could not stop it, hinder it, or overpower it!

A Word of Warning

It is precisely these four areas the adversary will attack so he can disrupt and, if possible, destroy the church. That's why it's important to keep our priorities straight. It's essential that we not get distracted by all that we *can* do as a church . . . and stay focused on only what we *must* do as a church. Otherwise, we may be attracting a crowd for the wrong reasons.

This emphasis on the essentials is what the apostle Paul had in mind when he passed on the torch of ministry to a young pastor named Timothy:

> I solemnly charge you in the presence of God and of Christ Jesus, who is to judge the living and the dead, and by His appearing and His kingdom: preach the word; be ready in season and out of season; reprove, rebuke, exhort, with great patience and instruction. For the time will come when they will not endure sound doctrine; but wanting to have their ears tickled, they will

accumulate for themselves teachers in accordance to their own desires, and will turn away their ears from the truth and will turn aside to myths. (2 Timothy 4:1–4)

Notice both the command and the reason for it. The command is clear: "preach the word"—followed by an explanation of *when* and *how* to do it. But there's also a *why*, a reason to proclaim boldly the Bible on a consistent basis: there will come a time when biblical truth will be rejected in favor of what people want to hear. The biblical alternative? According to Acts 6:1–7, the Lord will honor and bless any plan that upholds prayer and promotes His Word. This is what Paul was affirming to Timothy.

Large numbers don't necessarily reveal God's blessing. They could, in fact, reveal error. They could reflect an ear-tickling ministry that panders to people and tells the crowds what they *want* to hear, instead of what they *need* to hear. A growing number of churches and denominations today have found the four essentials unnecessary—burdensome, you might say. Archaic traditions of a bygone era. So they have hired what I call "pulpit whores," or put more mildly, "teachers in accordance to their own desires"—to affirm them in their selfish and carnal lifestyles.

No wonder the crowds expand . . . it's as if God has officially approved their sin!

But even a calloused conscience eventually aches with the emptiness that only God—the true God—can fill. The tragedy is that these empty individuals think they have already tried God . . . and He has left them just as unfulfilled as the world has. It's downright tragic.

Our culture is driven by marketing. There's no escaping it. Consumerism and materialism have wormed their way into our lives, and marketing spreads the disease. For instance, how can I know which of the eight hundred cereals in the store is most healthful? Which car should I purchase? What vacation should we take this summer? See the dilemma? Consumers must make decisions. How can we possibly determine what to buy with so many options to choose from, with so little money to spend, and with such limited time to spare? Marketing informs us which choices will make us most comfortable . . . bring the most satisfaction . . . cause the least inconvenience . . . give us the biggest bang for our buck . . . and the like. You get the picture.

I've learned through the years that perception overshadows reality. I hate that, but it's true. From political candidates to polyester carpet, how people perceive things is, to them, more convincing than a truckload of evidence. Unfortunately, most people draw their opinions from the shallow stream of perception instead of the deep reservoir of truth. I find that strange and disappointing.

Marketing works. That's why each year businesses spend billions of dollars trying to get us to spend just as much. In his book *The Brand Gap*, marketing guru Marty Neumeier offers a number of strategies to help companies develop and protect their unique brands. But he also offers a witty insight into a deeper motivation for consumer purchases:

> Depending on your Unique Buying State, you can join any number of tribes on any number of days and feel part of something bigger than yourself. You can belong to the Callaway tribe when you play golf, the VW tribe when you drive to work, and the Williams-Sonoma tribe when you cook a meal. You're part of a select clan (or so you feel) when you buy products from these clearly differentiated companies. Brands are the little gods of modern life, each ruling a different need, activity, mood, or situation.

> Yet you're in control. If your latest god
> falls from Olympus, you can switch to
> another one.[4]

This example was written tongue-in-cheek, of course, but it taps a profound need. Often we make decisions—both large and small—in an attempt to satisfy something deep within ourselves. This truth motivates more than spending. Even our critical life decisions are often made based on a consumer mind-set. Scary thought, isn't it? Perception actually overshadows reality.

It's even more frightening when we realize that our culture doesn't market Christianity very well. Have you ever noticed it's usually the aberrant "Christian"—preferably an evangelical—the media displays to represent the rest of us? Like William Jennings Bryan at the Scopes Monkey trial, this poor individual is revealed in all his or her pitiful naïveté, promptly vilified, pigeonholed, and finally, dismissed with a laugh. Christianity looks foolish. Perception overshadows reality.

Then, at other times, when controversial subjects like abortion, homosexuality, evolution, or the inerrancy of the Scriptures find their way to prime-time debates, the "Christian" view is usually defended by some theological liberal who couldn't tell the book of Genesis from Boy George. This "expert" only quotes verses about the love of God and calls no one to any standard. It's the theological liberal the world embraces in a politically correct culture. It's the Bible-believing, evangelical Christian, however, whom our tolerant world cannot tolerate.

Our culture has branded evangelicals as narrow exclusivists, hypocritical killjoys, and religious fanatics. In short, we're oddballs. (Not a great brand.) Who wants to be an oddball? Moreover, who wants to go to an oddball church?

Aware of our stereotype, we evangelicals find it tempting to fight fire with fire . . . or marketing with marketing. "Our church is not boring," we promise. "This is *not* your grandmother's church," we assure the younger generation. But we need to be careful with our words . . . fighting fire with fire could be dangerous. Tyler Wigg-Stevenson, a Baptist preacher and author, writes in an article titled "Jesus Is Not a Brand":

> Marketing is not a values-neutral language. Marketing unavoidably changes the message—as all media do. Why? Because marketing is the particular vernacular of a consumerist society in which everything has

a price tag. To market something
is therefore to effectively make
it into a branded product to be
consumed. . . . And we market the
church at our peril if we are blind to
the critical and categorical difference
between the Truth and a truth you
can sell. In a marketing culture, the
Truth becomes a product. People
will encounter it with the same consumerist worldview with which they
encounter every other product in the
American marketplace.[5]

Most people would never intentionally
compare Jesus to Coca-Cola or Chevrolet. But
in a consumerist society, we run the danger of
implying that the good news of Jesus is just one
of many similar choices, all of which are equally
valid. Just choose your flavor of Savior. But Jesus
never gave us that option. He claimed that He was
the *only way* to God the Father (see John 14:6). In
a world that's bound for hell, Jesus's claim isn't
selfish exclusivism. It's grace.

Our world has lost its way. So it's no surprise
that when the church takes its cues from the
world, the church begins to go astray as well.
But must we resort to gimmicks for people to
come to church? Is biblical reinterpretation the

new essential for church growth? Must we dumb down historic Christianity into shallow entertainment in order to pamper consumers? May it never be! I am convinced that the church doesn't need marketing devices, worldly strategies, live entertainment, or a corporate mentality to be contagious. Not if the glory of God is the goal. Not if the growth of God's people is in view. Rather, the church needs biblical truth taught correctly and clearly . . . and lived out in authenticity.

One of the worst things we can do in our churches is take our eyes off the essentials — take our cues of how to "do church" from our postmodern world instead of determining our distinctives and priorities from the Scriptures. It's a great temptation to try that these days, because there are so many churches doing it. They look like they know what they're doing. The crowds swell. The ratings soar. The money pours in. They speak in such a convincing way that we are tempted to think, *Well, maybe they're right, and we're missing it.* Please. Don't go there.

As we're beginning to think about the essentials of a healthy church, we need to define what it is that makes it contagious. How should a church grow biblically? What environment causes a community to take notice? It isn't just the building, or the sound system, or the music. It's not even the preaching. I repeat, it's the context that makes a church contagious.

It's the people.

And it's more than the numbers of people. It's their passion. It's their Spirit-directed enthusiasm. It's the obvious work of God engaging the lives of believers in meaningful connection, genuine compassion, and almost electric excitement about reaching out into the community and investing themselves wholeheartedly into places of ministry.

Let me say it again. When considering church growth, we must think strategically, we must preach creatively, and our worship must connect. Absolutely. But we must also be careful. A marketing mentality and a consumer mind-set have no business in the church of Jesus Christ. By that I mean, Jesus is *not* a brand . . . human thinking does *not* guide God's work . . . and the church is *not* a corporation. The church of Jesus Christ is a *spiritual entity*, guided by the Lord through the precepts of His Word.

If we sacrifice the essentials of *teaching, fellowship, breaking of bread*, and *prayer* on the altar of strategy, creativity, entertainment, and "relevancy," we abandon the main reasons the church exists. We should *build on* those essentials, not attempt to replace them.

Four Characteristics of a Contagious Church

Now that we've laid the foundation, let's examine four characteristics of a contagious ministry, all from Paul's last letter to Timothy.

A Place of Grace

Paul underscores the principles of a contagious church with four verbs. As we interpret the Scriptures, we should always pay attention to the verbs in a passage. Verbs are the backbone of literature. They hold thoughts together. When there is action to be taken, verbs reveal the steps we must walk to align ourselves with truth. In this case, the verbs appear as commands required to nurture a church environment that is both biblical and attractive. Here's the first one:

> You therefore, my son, be strong
> in the grace that is in Christ Jesus.
> (2 Timothy 2:1)

From the verb *be strong*, we glean the first characteristic for a contagious church: *it is always necessary to be strong in grace*. That sounds simple, but it is one of the most difficult principles to apply in a consumerist culture.

Where does the application of this principle begin? With church leaders. Paul could write this command because he himself modeled it. He proclaimed grace. He promoted grace. His message was the gospel of grace. He relied on grace. Paul never forgot the importance of God's unmerited favor in his own life . . . and it permeated his entire ministry. Read a sampling of Paul's own words:

> For all have sinned and fall short of the glory of God, being justified as a gift by His grace through the redemption which is in Christ Jesus. (Romans 3:23–24)

> For by grace you have been saved through faith; and that not of yourselves, it is the gift of God. (Ephesians 2:8)

> But when the kindness of God our Savior and His love for mankind appeared, He saved us, not on the

basis of deeds which we have done in righteousness, but according to His mercy, by the washing of regeneration and renewing by the Holy Spirit, whom He poured out upon us richly through Jesus Christ our Savior, so that being justified by His grace we would be made heirs according to the hope of eternal life. (Titus 3:4–7)

Isn't it amazing that this former legalistic Pharisee — this violent man whose life was once characterized by making sure that Christians were wiped out — was stopped in his tracks by grace? While on the road to Damascus, Paul was made blind by a light from heaven as the Lord Jesus spoke to him and called him (of all people!) into His work. That changed Paul from the inside out: the long-standing legalist was transformed into a messenger of grace! Paul's ministry emphasized grace to the lost as well as to those in God's family. As I've studied the life of Paul, I have found grace woven like a silver thread through the colorful tapestry of his ministry. Paul became the preeminent spokesman for grace:

Let it be known to you, brethren, that through Him forgiveness of sins is proclaimed to you, and through

Him everyone who believes is freed from all things, from which you could not be freed through the Law of Moses. (Acts 13:38–39)

Paul's message offered the good news of grace to the lost. This is the first part of Christ's Great Commission to the church (see Matthew 28:18–20). Imagine the impact our churches would have on our communities if each Christian committed to sharing the gospel of God's great grace once a week with someone who expresses a need. The lost need to hear how they can cross the bridge from a life filled with emptiness and guilt to a life flowing with mercy and peace and forgiveness . . . all because of His grace. We help build this bridge when we lovingly and patiently communicate the gospel.

You don't need a seminary degree. You don't have to know a lot of the religious vocabulary or the nuances of theology. In your own authentic, honest, and unguarded manner, simply share with people what Christ has done for you. Who knows? It may not be long before you will know the joy of leading a lost person from the darkness of death's dungeon across the bridge to the liberating hope of new life in Christ. How exciting . . . how *contagious*!

There's another reason being strong in grace makes a church attractive—the absence of legalism. Just as the lost don't understand the good news of Christ, so the saved rarely understand the remarkable reality of grace. I know of nothing more exhausting and less rewarding than Christians attempting to please the people around them by maintaining impossible legalistic demands. What a tragic trap, and the majority of believers are caught in it. When will we ever learn? Grace has set us free! That message streams throughout the sermons and personal testimonies of the apostle Paul.

Author Steve Brown says that some people think legalistic churches are as bad as grace-oriented churches. As he put it, these types of churches are no more alike than a taxidermist and a veterinarian. Some would claim, "Well, either way you get your dog back!" True, but one dog collects dust and never moves. The other is busy and barking and eating and jumping . . . he's *alive!* He's the real thing! The point? Let's choose to be veterinarians. Let's determine that our churches will be places of grace. A church of grace is alive, anticipating God's work, willing to risk, free of judgmentalism . . . but make no mistake—it's not free of holiness. There's a vast difference.

Once people trust in Jesus for the forgiveness of sins, we need to release them. Release them into the magnificent freedom grace provides. I don't mean leave them alone without biblical instruction or guidance. (We'll talk about that later.) I mean don't smother them with a boatload of *nonbiblical* rules and regulations that put them on probation and keep them in some holding tank until they "get their lives straightened out." Rules about what to wear, what to look like, what to eat and drink, what entertainment to enjoy, what movies Jesus would watch . . . et cetera. *Please.* That's a straitjacket of religious bondage. That's not a contagious place. It's a frightening place. The day a church stops being strong in grace is the day that church loses its magnetism. Truth sets people free (see John 8:32). Tragically, legalistic churches incarcerate them behind bars of fear.

When Paul stood on Mars Hill in Athens and proclaimed the grace of God to the lost, he preached to a crowd of skeptics, critics, and those we might call sophisticated eggheads. Rather than beginning with the Scriptures, Paul began with the created world in which these nonbelievers lived in order to introduce Jesus to them. He began with their spiritual hunger and pointed them to Jesus as the satisfaction for their longings . . . and the payment for their sins. Paul even quoted a pagan poet as a means of building a bridge between the lost and the Lord (see Acts 17:16–33).

A number of ministries and movements have adopted what I call a "Mars Hill philosophy of ministry." Modeled after Paul's message on Mars Hill, their goal is to connect with the nonbeliever, or the postmodern, or one they would call a "seeker." In recent years, the "emerging" church movement has attempted to "do church" (or *be* the church) in a new way amid our postmodern world. Their purpose is "missional living," that is, to get involved in the world in hopes of transforming it. This style of ministry engages the culture in a "conversation," rather than preaches to people as a prophet. A wide range of theologies and strategies exist within this current movement. Some individuals hold to orthodox beliefs but have adopted very unorthodox ways of communication. I have read of sermons that use language that would make most believers cringe . . . and cover their children's ears.[6]

Are we to minister as those *in the world*? Absolutely. That's an answer to Jesus's own prayer for His followers (see John 17:14–16). But let's be very discerning here. Does this mean we must minister as those *of the world*? Do we have to adopt postmodern thinking in order to minister to the postmodern mind? *Absolutely not.* Such behavior and words are not fitting in the life of a Christian (see Ephesians 5:4). They are obviously, then, not fitting in the context of worship.

Please understand, grace does not mean anything goes, which includes biblical theology. One author, who likens the emerging church to the Protestant Reformation, writes,

> The actual nature of the Atonement . . . or the tenet of an angry God who must be appeased on the question of evil's origins are suddenly all up for reconsideration. If in pursuing this line of exegesis, the Great Emergence really does what most of its observers think it will, it will rewrite Christian theology—and thereby North American culture—into something far more Jewish, more paradoxical, more narrative, and more mystical than anything the Church has had for the last seventeen or eighteen hundred years.[7]

Is this what grace requires of us? Since when was the nature of the Atonement determined by anything other than a close, careful examination of the Scriptures? When the inerrant Word of God is not our standard for truth, erosion will creep in. It will eventually crowd out truth. David Wells offers a helpful reminder:

> Scripture is divine revelation. It is not a collection of opinions of how different people see things that tells us more about the people than the things. No. It gives us God's perfect knowledge of himself and of all reality. It is given to us in a form we can understand. The reason God gave it to us is that he wants us to know. Not to guess. Not to have vague impressions. And certainly not to be misled. He wants us to know. It is not immodest, nor arrogant, to claim that we know, when what we know is what God had given us to know through his Word.[8]

I need to make this clear: I don't intend to erect an "emerging" straw man and then light him on fire. I realize, in the same way our culture unfairly pigeonholes evangelicals, there is a risk of stereotyping the emerging church—or any similar movement. The danger of a broad stroke of analysis is to fail to represent everyone fairly or to recognize the exceptions. I'm certain that not all of those who number themselves among the "tribe" of the emerging church favor liberal theology with no belief in absolutes or traditional, orthodox convictions. However, my concern is for those churches *in any movement* that, in an attempt to connect with the culture, actually embrace a compromise of biblical truth. Paul had the same concern as he wrote with urgency to Timothy. Take a look at this verse once again.

> I solemnly charge you in the presence of God and of Christ Jesus, who is to judge the living and the dead, and by His appearing and His kingdom: preach the word; be ready in season and out of season; reprove, rebuke, exhort, with great patience and instruction. (2 Timothy 4:1–2)

In other words, stick with the plan God has promised to bless and use: preaching the timeless, ever-relevant, always-powerful Word. Deliver the biblical goods! Stick with Scripture. Be strong in the grace that is in Christ Jesus. It's worth noticing that this exhortation is not addressed to the hearer; it's for the speaker. The one who is to obey this command is the one proclaiming the message. That's your pastor. That's me. That's every elder who teaches. That's all who are called to stand and deliver. It is to be the commitment of every church. That's a crucial part of being a place of grace . . . a contagious church. Being strong in grace always begins with the leadership.

Methods may differ, and taste in music may fluctuate. But there's an appropriate limit churches must recognize. Churches don't need to try so hard to be so creative and cute that folks miss the truth. No need for meaningless and silly substitutes that dumb down God's Word. These may entertain people—even encourage them—but rarely will they convict the lost or bring believers deeper in their maturity. Teaching the truth takes care of all that. Remember Paul's words: "Reprove, rebuke, exhort" (2 Timothy 4:2). Those are not politically correct terms. Why? Because God is not politically correct. He never intended to be.

Sadly, in an alarming number of churches today, God's people are being told what they *want* to hear rather than what they *need* to hear. They are being spoon-fed warm milk, not challenged to digest solid meat. A watered-down teaching ministry will usually attract crowds (for a while), but it has no eternal impact. Jesus chose and appointed us that we may bear fruit that lasts (see John 15:16). Even Jesus, by teaching the politically *incorrect* truth (but the truth nonetheless), lost some followers (see John 6:66). Nothing wrong with that. I've not been able to find any place in the Scriptures where God expresses the least bit of concern for enlarging the size of an audience as the goal of the church. Satisfying the curious, scratching the itching ears of our postmodern audiences, is an exercise in futility. Like eating cotton candy, the experience may be delightful . . . but there's no food value. David Wells offers another helpful insight:

> The truth is that without a biblical understanding of why God instituted it, the church easily becomes a liability in a market where it competes only with the greatest of difficulty against religious fare available in the convenience of one's living room and in a culture bent on distraction and entertainment. . . . The evangelical church, or at least a good slice of it, is nervous, twitchy, and touchy about consumer desire, ready to change in a nanosecond at the slightest hint that tastes and interests have changed. Why? Because consumer appetite reigns.[9]

There is a major problem with adapting a church to fit the lost person, rather than the church following God's design for what He intended it to be. Here it is, plain and simple: the church is a body of people *called out* from among the world for the distinct and unique purpose of glorifying their Savior and Lord. Nowhere in the book of Acts or the Epistles do we see a church called to provide a subculture for nonbelievers. The lost don't need to find at church a world that's like their world outside the church. The church is not competing with the world. Jesus is not a brand.

The church needs to guard against compromising the Word of God so that it tastes more palatable to newcomers. Christians suffer when we make that kind of compromise. I've said for years, "Sermonettes are for Christianettes." If our churches give little eight-minute sermons, we are not feeding the flock. Instead of teaching them, we're tantalizing them. Instead of stretching and challenging them, we're entertaining them. Our congregations need pastors who study hard, pray hard, and prepare well-balanced meals, then open the Scriptures and teach people how to study the Word for themselves. That's what gives them stability in hard times, discernment in the midst of deception, and the strength to stand alone.

But like Joshua Bell in the subway, it takes more than a gift expressed with skill to make a church contagious. It takes a context. It takes an entire church functioning as a place of grace . . . with leaders setting the pace.

In late 2007, Pastor Bill Hybels and the leadership team of the Willow Creek Community Church shared the startling results of a study they conducted of their own church — as well as other so-called seeker churches. The results, Hybels said, were "the greatest wake-up call of my adult life." Among other findings, they discovered that their ministry to "seekers" was very effective for introducing Christ to those who were new to church. No big surprise. But they had not been as successful in fulfilling their mission statement to turn "irreligious people into fully devoted followers of Christ." That is, they had not been as strong in developing the spiritual lives of those who had trusted Christ. In a conversation Hybels had with his executive pastor, Greg Hawkins, they realized this:

> We should have started telling people and teaching people that they have to take responsibility to become self-feeders. . . . We should have taught people how to read their

Bibles between services, how to do the spiritual practices. . . . What's happening to these people [is that] the older they get, the more they're expecting the church to feed them, when, in fact, the more mature a Christian becomes, a Christian should become more of a self-feeder. . . . We're going to up the level of responsibility we put on the people themselves so that they can grow even if the church doesn't meet all their needs.[10]

I admire Bill for his vulnerability and candor. I applaud any church that takes spiritual growth seriously enough to evaluate its effectiveness and to modify its methods of discipleship to the biblical model. If only *all* churches would periodically take a long look into the mirror of God's Word! In fact, if evaluation is not done on a regular basis, erosion *will* occur. It can happen anywhere; I know that for a fact.

Allow me to talk directly to church leaders for a moment. Let me urge you who are considering adopting the emerging church philosophy, or the "seeker church" strategies, to take a good look at what you are trying to do—*and why.*

Be sure to look at it biblically. Be certain you can support any change you plan to implement from the Scriptures. Don't look to Mars Hill in Acts 17 while ignoring the essentials of Acts 2. Instead of searching for justification in the Bible, search and pray for direction from the biblical text. Then follow it. I would say the same thing to *any* church, including my own.

A place of grace releases and affirms; it doesn't smother. Grace values the dignity of individuals; it doesn't destroy. Grace supports and encourages; it isn't jealous or suspicious. In the church, grace is the means by which the gospel is preached. But it also becomes the *context* where God's written commands are taught. Here's how Paul puts it:

> For the grace of God has appeared, bringing salvation to all men, instructing us to deny ungodliness and worldly desires and to live sensibly, righteously and godly in the present age, looking for the blessed hope and the appearing of the glory of our great God and Savior, Christ Jesus, who gave Himself for us to redeem us from every lawless deed, and to purify for Himself a people

for His own possession, zealous
for good deeds. These things speak
and exhort and reprove with all
authority. Let no one disregard you.
(Titus 2:11–15)

Did you notice, "the grace of God has
appeared . . . instructing us to deny ungodli-
ness"? I repeat it only to underscore: grace doesn't
mean anything goes. Rather, grace motivates our
behavior. Grace frees us to obey. Being strong in
grace goes hand in hand with being committed
to living the truth. There is no contradiction
in those two commitments. After all, "grace
and truth were realized through Jesus Christ"
(John 1:17). Grace provides the context for God's
commands to be taught. Truth equips our minds
and shapes up our lives. Truth, therefore, must
be taught! That brings us to the second characteristic of a contagious church.

A Place of Mentoring

Jesus gave the church its marching orders in
practical terms. You're probably familiar with His
words:

> Go therefore and make disciples of
> all the nations, baptizing them in
> the name of the Father and the Son

and the Holy Spirit, teaching them
to observe all that I commanded
you; and lo, I am with you
always, even to the end of the age.
(Matthew 28:19–20)

Here in Jesus's Great Commission to His
followers, we find no greater challenge . . . and
no more comforting promise. But you probably
have never considered the Great Commission
as part of what makes a church contagious. The
command to "make disciples" has two parts. The
first, "baptizing them," assumes that we'll share
our faith with the lost. The second, "teaching
them to observe," directs us to share our lives
of faith with those who have believed in Jesus.
Returning to the second chapter of Paul's final
letter to Timothy, we see the practical outworking
of how the Lord intends this "teaching" to occur:

The things which you have heard
from me in the presence of many
witnesses, entrust these to faithful
men who will be able to teach others
also. (2 Timothy 2:2)

This verse offers us our second characteristic:
*churches that are contagious faithfully mentor those
who are coming along in the Christian life.* The verb

that gives us this direction is *entrust*. The term literally means to hand over "something to someone . . . for safekeeping." [11] I like that image. We invest the truth like a trust in the lives of others. We have a valuable message we pass along to others.

Paul's words to Timothy outline a process of multiplication that can be visualized in a simple chart:

Paul → *Timothy* → *faithful men and women* → *others also*

Paul the apostle entrusted his heart, soul, truths, confrontations, encouragements, affirmations — his very life — to Timothy. Timothy was a recipient, much like the second runner in a relay receives the baton from the first runner. Timothy then looked for others to pass that baton on to — those who would be faithful to pass it along to others also. This process has been occurring since Jesus began it with His apostles, including Paul. In fact, we are all recipients of Paul's baton. Duane Litfin, former president of Wheaton College, calls this "the endless chain of Christian discipleship." The Navigators call this "the ministry of multiplication." Both are correct. It is an essential part of a contagious church.

A church is not just a gathering of people who sit and listen to one person preach. As important as the message is, it is only part of the passing of the baton. One person's life touches the life of another, who then touches the lives of people in his or her sphere of influence—those whom the originator would never have known. To make it even more exciting, those recipients, in turn, touch the lives of others also. *That* is a contagious ministry.

The medical profession models the idea of multiplication very well. They don't just educate and graduate medical students and then cut them loose, saying, "Okay, folks, lots of luck. Carve away!" How would you like to be a patient lying on the bed, about to go in for surgery, and the doctor blurts, "You know, I've never really actually done surgery, but hey, we'll give it the ol' college try. Turn on the anesthesia, Doc . . . and let's get 'er done!" You'd explode, "*Wait! Stop!*" Why? You want somebody who's been trained. *Really* trained. You want a skilled surgeon, one who has traveled across the country to study under the most outstanding doctor in his or her field. You want a professional, who has learned specific, tried-and-true techniques of doing medical work correctly—one who has spent years being shaped, observed, confronted, reproved, rebuked, and corrected. In a word, you need someone who has been *mentored.*

Any education is most effective when the teachers are more than mere dispensers of information. Students need a school where the professors care about the *lives* of their students, where a student is not just number 314 in the class. That's why I don't believe a theological education can take place online. (You don't learn surgery online, by the way.) *Information* can go on the Web, but an *education* requires more than data. It involves the touch of a mentor — one seasoned life poured into another inexperienced life.

Why do I say this with such conviction? I am the product of mentoring. There have been men in my life, some of whom you would not know if I mentioned their names, who have made a major difference in my life. They saw potential where I did not. They encouraged me to become something more than I was. They reproved and corrected me. They modeled what I longed to become. One of the first of these men saw the most potential in me where I saw the least.

When I began high school, I stuttered so badly I could not finish a sentence. With that speech impediment came a very low self-esteem. I learned to keep my mouth shut and maintain a low profile. The *last* place I wanted to be was in front of an audience! I managed to get through the first weeks of my freshman year without embarrassing myself too often when, one day, Dick Nieme found me at my hall locker and shocked me with his words: "Chuck, I want you on my debate team. I'd also like you to take one of my elective courses in dramatic arts."

"Who, m-m-m-m-m-m-me?" I looked over my shoulder at the guy standing behind me. I thought for sure Dr. Nieme was talking to him. "Y-y-y-y-y-y-you want hi-him. You d-d-don't want m-me."

"No, I know who I want. I want you. You've got the right stuff, young man. We just need to tap into it." I finally gave in . . . very reluctantly. Starting the very next week, Dr. Nieme met with me from 7:15 to 7:45 each morning before school for speech therapy sessions. Very common now. Almost unheard of back then. He helped me understand that my mind was running ahead of my ability to form the words in my mouth properly. My mind was running ahead of my mouth. (I have the *opposite* problem now.) He taught me to slow down, pace my thoughts, and concentrate on starting the words I wanted to say. He gave me exercises to hone my enunciation and give a rhythm for each syllable to follow. I joined the debate team . . . and, ultimately, I loved it! That led to my participating in school plays. Our drama team jelled into a top-notch bunch of young actors. We went on to enter the finals of the Texas state one-act play competition. What a blast! I hardly need to tell you, Dick Nieme was there all the way. When I failed, he coached and encouraged. At each triumph, he applauded louder than anyone else in the audience. He challenged me and inspired me, and we continued to set goals just beyond my reach.

Finally, I auditioned for the lead role in the senior play . . . and landed it. When the curtain rose that night, Dick Nieme sat front row, balcony. When I came out for my bow, he was the first to stand . . . again, he cheered the loudest. He really embarrassed me . . . but I loved it. Today, more than fifty-five years later, I look back and realize how much I owe that man. He believed in me. He respected me. He started me down the path to becoming the man—the preacher—that God intended. I'm glad I was able to express my deep gratitude to him before he died. I'm glad he knew the impact he had on at least one life. I'm honored to have been invited to write his eulogy. I still give God thanks for that mentor.

The church becomes a place of mentoring when we stop seeing people as heads to count and money to collect. Instead, we view people as opportunities to build into their lives. In Paul's letter to Titus, the apostle spoke in similar terms of multiplication, just as he did with Timothy. Notice how more than information is passed on from person to person. Mentoring involves the modeling of character:

> Older women likewise are to be reverent in their behavior, not malicious gossips nor enslaved to much wine, teaching what is good, so that they may encourage the young women to love their husbands, to love their children, to be sensible, pure, workers at home, kind, being subject to their own husbands, so that the word of God will not be dishonored. (Titus 2:3–5)

Another of my mentors, Howard Hendricks, says that every Christian needs at least three individuals in his or her life. We need someone who has come before us who mentors us. We need another beside us who shares our burden. And we need someone beyond us whom we're mentoring. Otherwise, we grow stagnant. The church then becomes a place where Christians sit, soak, and sour. They take notes, walk out, and come back next week . . . to sit, take notes, walk out, and return again next week . . . to sit, take more notes, and walk out . . . until (ho-hum) Jesus comes back. What's wrong with that picture? *Virtually everything!* There's no contagion. No application and change, personally. No passing of the baton. No multiplication. Just stagnation. I know of no one who says it clearer than Dr. Hendricks in his fine volume *Standing Together: Impacting Your Generation*. See if you catch a glimpse of yourself in his words:

> Many of us in the church are under the mistaken impression that the way to produce spiritually mature Christians is to enroll people in a course on spiritual maturity. We give them books on the subject. We take them to passages of Scripture. We hand out assignments and worksheets. Nothing wrong with these activities. But has it ever occurred to you that spiritual growth is rarely the product of assimilating more information? If it were, we could have transformed the world several million books ago. But inasmuch as knowing Christ involves a *relationship*, growing in Christ also involves relationships. One of the

most helpful of these involves a mentor. That's because most of us don't need to know more nearly as much as we need to *be known* more. We don't need a set of principles to practice nearly as much as we need another *person* to help us. We need someone to believe in us, stand by us, guide us, model Christ for us. We need another's encouragement, wisdom, example, and accountability. We need his smiles, his hugs, his frowns, his tears. . . . People will forget most of what you say; they will forget almost nothing of what you do. Therefore, whatever behavior you model for your protégé is the pattern he will tend to follow—or, in some cases, reject.[12]

Make no mistake, we all need mentors. Furthermore, we all need those we are mentoring. The church is the ideal place to connect both. When it does, it becomes a contagious place. Just as the home is the place where life training takes place, so the church is another family of sorts—a spiritual family. I read an article that mentioned the fact that 90 percent of the ministries that target a younger generation—for example, Generation X—ran into trouble after only three years.[13] Why? For one reason, because these age-targeted ministries often separate young adults from other age-groups in the church.

A contagious church comprises a body of caring women and men who see value in others and take the time to cultivate those lives. That must become a goal in our churches. Otherwise the church becomes a dusty old museum full of stuffed Christians, straight from the taxidermist. When the church fails to reproduce . . . it dies.

Webster defines a *mentor* as "a trusted counselor or guide; tutor, coach."[14] This describes a man I knew during a vulnerable time in my life as a young man. I was serving in the Marine Corps, stationed on the island of Okinawa . . . separated from my newlywed wife for about seventeen long, lonely months. I arrived at that island disheartened and disillusioned. I left transformed. The difference-maker? A mentor.

To my surprise, Bob Newkirk, a representative for the Navigators, took an interest in me as a person. We regularly played handball, ate meals, prayed, and played together. I stayed in his home on occasion. I spent holidays there when I was off duty on liberty. Bob and I did street meetings together. At those gatherings, I would lead singing, and Bob would preach. We ministered as a team. I went through an advanced

Scripture-memory program, thanks to Bob. He confronted me. He pointed out blind spots. He built into my life. He loved me. I decided to return to advance my education, enter seminary, and pursue a lifetime of ministry through his influence. *That* is mentoring.

The sermons I preach, the books I write, the life I model to my family and congregation all are a direct result of mentors who have poured their lives into my life. It's their lives and the truth of Scripture that they passed on to me in mentoring that I pass along to others in my life.

I've discovered when individuals are young and unusually gifted, the most common tendency is to drift toward arrogance and, sometimes, raw conceit. Almost without exception when I detect conceit in an individual, I say to myself, *They haven't been mentored.* I have never met a self-important, arrogant individual who has been well mentored. Truth be told, arrogance doesn't survive mentoring. A mentor will point out blind spots and will reprove you appropriately when you need to be confronted about your pride. And a mentor won't back off. He or she relentlessly presses for excellence.

A church that's contagious cares enough about people to build into their lives. Never forget that. As a result of being mentored, an individual learns the value of being vulnerable, open, unguarded, honest, and, ideally, a person of authenticity.

A Place of Hardship . . . and Fellowship

There's a third characteristic of a contagious church. It involves the realities of life we often mask behind pride and — may I say it? — hypocrisy. Everybody hurts. But not everybody lives an honest and vulnerable life that admits the pain. Why? Very often, there isn't a safe place to do so. The church should be that place (second only to the home).

I heard of a research study where psychologists discovered the top three places where average people "fake it." First, we tend to put on airs when we visit the lobby of a fancy hotel. Next, we typically fake our true feelings alongside the salesperson at a new-car showroom. And the third place we wear a mask? You guessed it. In church!

Tragically, in church, where there should be authenticity, we'll paint on the phony smiles, slap backs, and masquerade to hide what is inside our hearts — the fact that in reality . . . we're hurting. I've often said if you could know the pain in the lives of those sitting in front of and behind you in church, you'd be shocked. Everybody hurts. We've all been shot . . . we're all bleeding within, including the one behind the pulpit. I love the insightful words of Dietrich Bonhoeffer:

> The pious fellowship permits no one to be a sinner. So everybody must conceal his sin from himself and from the fellowship. We dare not be sinners. Many Christians are unthinkably horrified when a real sinner is suddenly discovered among the righteous. So we remain alone with our sin, living in lies and hypocrisy. The fact is that we *are* sinners! But it is the grace of the Gospel, which is so hard for the pious to understand, that it confronts us with the truth and says: You are a sinner, a great, desperate sinner; now come, as the sinner that you are, to God who loves you. He wants you as you are; He does not want anything from you, a sacrifice, a work; He wants you alone. "My son, give me thine heart" (Prov. 23:26). God has come to you to save the sinner. Be glad! This message is liberation through truth. You can hide nothing from God. The

mask you wear before men will do you no good before Him. He wants to see you as you are, He wants to be gracious to you. You do not have to go on lying to yourself and your brothers, as if you were without sin; you can dare to be a sinner. Thank God for that; He loves the sinner but hates sin.[15]

Part of what makes a church an attractive place is when Christians aren't afraid to live transparent lives with one another. Paul's challenge to Timothy pushes past the facade and reminds us to live in reality:

> Suffer hardship with me, as a good soldier of Christ Jesus. (2 Timothy 2:3)

I like the simplicity of Paul's words . . . though they are not simple to live. In the original Greek language, the phrase "Suffer hardship with me" translates a single verb, *sugkakopatheson*, which means, "to endure the same kind of suffering as others."[16] It's not a command we can obey on our own. It requires the application of a third characteristic of a contagious church: *when tested the body pulls closer together.* What a blessing it is when this actually occurs! See the word *with* in the verse? That's what makes a church attractive to others. When one hurts, we all hurt. Nobody hurts solo.

I am privileged to be a part of a church that has people who care. We even have a group called Soul Care—it's made up of everyday, garden-variety folks who come alongside others in times of extreme difficulty. Some in our congregation are struggling through ugly, unwanted divorces. Others are victims of rape. Some have been abused. There are some gripped with lingering, debilitating addictions. A number have loved ones who have special needs. Many churches will help these folks find the exit when they have these challenges. (I'm not kidding; I've seen it occur!) Instead, we welcome them. We want to help them work through the difficulties. We suffer *with* them. I don't mean to sound like we've got it all together. No, it's not that . . . but we do pull together, albeit imperfectly. How can that happen? We're back to that great truth: grace. Grace constantly reminds us that the ground at the foot of the cross is level.

It's like what occurred in the early church. Who would have ever thought so many Christians would have been martyred? Because of the persecution, the church pressed right on. Because they suffered together, their ranks grew. You don't find that in the world's system. When testing comes, folks usually scatter like rats on a sinking ship; it's every man for himself! There's competition. There's envy. It's all about the almighty dollar. But in the church? Grace pulls us together. It's about considering others more important than ourselves. When someone is going through a tough time, a phone call is made. Somebody shows up at his or her door. Someone brings a bag or two of groceries . . . sometimes a hot meal. You cannot suffer hardship with someone from a distance. In a contagious church, everybody hurts. But nobody hurts or heals alone.

This is one reason I find the prosperity gospel movement so heretical. Nowhere in the New Testament do you find God promising health, wealth, and prosperity to those who have enough faith. That way of thinking is a direct result of consumerism-Christianity. You don't see it in the early church or anywhere in the New Testament Letters. Even the life of Jesus—One who had *complete* faith—was a life of struggle that ended with crucifixion! He was "a man of sorrows and acquainted with grief" (Isaiah 53:3). How's that for prosperity? "When Christ calls a man," writes Dietrich Bonhoeffer, "He bids him come and die." [17] The normal Christian life is a cross-bearing life. It's the *next* life that promises health and prosperity. To say otherwise is to misrepresent the message of Christ, personally, and the New Testament as a whole.

The apostle Paul illustrates what he means by suffering hardship together by using three metaphors:

> No soldier in active service entangles himself in the affairs of everyday life, so that he may please the one who enlisted him as a soldier. Also if anyone competes as an athlete, he does not win the prize unless he competes according to the rules. The hard-working farmer ought to be the first to receive his share of the crops.
> (2 Timothy 2:4–6)

What great analogies! A soldier . . . an athlete . . . a farmer. The soldier reminds us that we're in a battle, and the battle requires a serious dedication to God alone. Whoever heard of a soldier working in the business world while carrying a weapon on foreign soil? He or she can't do that. There's a fight to fight. In his *Address to Martyrs*, the church father Tertullian wrote,

> No soldier comes to the war sur-rounded by luxuries, nor goes into

action from a comfortable bedroom,
but from the makeshift/narrow tent,
where pleasantness is to be found.

I love the way author Warren Wiersbe puts it:

> Christian service means invading
> a battleground, not a playground;
> and you and I are the weapons God
> uses to attack and defeat the enemy.
> When God used Moses' rod, He
> needed Moses' hand to lift it. When
> God used David's sling, He needed
> David's hand to swing it. When God
> builds a ministry, He needs some-
> body's surrendered body to get the
> job done.[18]

In a way similar to a soldier, an athlete
focuses and devotes himself or herself to the
task. Evidently, Paul was a sports fan, for
he used this metaphor more than once (see
1 Corinthians 9:25). While every event had
its prize, each one also had its rules. The athlete had to compete "according to the rules."
The original term for *rules* refers to "lawfully"
participating. God has left us with boundaries,
and we're to live within them. Holiness. Purity
of motive. Discipline. Self-control. A servant's

heart. Integrity in private as well as in public. Perseverance to the end. Just like an athlete running. Tough stuff!

Paul's illustration of the farmer emphasizes the labor that accompanies any meaningful ministry. It never just happens. Blessings from God rest upon ministries that remain actively engaged in serving Him. That calls for hard work. And it often goes unnoticed. I've never seen a group of people out in a farmer's field applauding and yelling, "Great job on the tractor! Wow, look how straight that row is! Keep it up; it will be worth it!" No, instead he does all the plowing and planting, but nobody's there to see it. He wipes the sweat off his brow with a bandanna, walks inside, washes up, and eats a huge meal . . . and never gains a pound. Why? He's a hardworking farmer. He diligently maintains his crops.

I stayed at the home of a farmer years ago when I was ministering in the San Joaquin Valley. Behind his home he had an orange orchard with trees *loaded* with oranges. One quiet morning we walked out back together and made our way into his orchard. I reached out and plucked a huge orange off a tree. "Man, look at that orange!" I said. "To think that just happened on its own."

The farmer reached and grabbed it out of my hand. "Give me that orange. That did not 'just happen.' Chuck, I pruned this tree. I sprayed this tree. I watered this tree. I watched this tree. I prayed over this tree. This orange did not 'just happen.' "

We had a good laugh over my stupid comment.

The hardworking farmer gets the job done. Is it any wonder why so many in our generation don't want to farm? It's terribly hard work . . . nothing easy about it. Neither is the suffering together that ministry requires. John R. W. Stott writes,

> This notion that Christian service is hard work is so unpopular in some happy-go-lucky Christian circles today that I feel the need to underline it. . . . The blessing of God rested upon the ministry of the apostle Paul in quite exceptional measure. . . . I find myself wondering if we attribute it sufficiently to the zeal and zest, the almost obsessional devotion, with which he gave himself to the work.[19]

We have hard work ahead of us as the body of Christ. That includes praying together as we've not prayed before. That includes laboring to make our fellowships places of grace. That includes pouring our lives into one another, mentoring those younger in the faith. It also means that we endure hardship with one another. Show me a church that is contagious, attracting people from far and wide, and I'll show you a group of Christians devoted to hard work—regardless of the cost. That brings us to the fourth and final distinctive.

A Place of Selfless Endurance

The last characteristic we'll examine can be summed up this way: *because of Jesus Christ, the church must endure every difficulty for the benefit of others*. I find this principle again in Paul's writings to Timothy:

> For this reason I endure all things for the sake of those who are chosen, so that they also may obtain the salvation which is in Christ Jesus and with it eternal glory. (2 Timothy 2:10)

The key to this principle is found in the verb *endure*. The term *hupomeno* is a compound word—from *hupo*, meaning "under," and *meno*, meaning, "to abide."[20] We are expected to "abide under." The idea is that a healthy church body continues to stand firm underneath the difficulty and suffering that faithfulness requires. We endure every difficulty. We hold together. We don't whine. We don't quit. Leaders don't resign just because things get tough. We keep our word. We aren't self-serving. We maintain our integrity. The reason? Paul tells us: "for the sake of those who are chosen, so that they also may obtain the salvation which is in Christ Jesus and with it eternal glory" (2 Timothy 2:10). We don't cave in to the culture or soften and lower the standard. We stay on message, and we consistently share that message with others. We don't drift from making Him known.

I like the story Charles Paul Conn tells in his book *Making It Happen*:

> When I lived in Atlanta, several years ago, I noticed in the *Yellow Pages*, in the listing of restaurants, an entry for a place called, Church of God Grill. The peculiar name aroused my curiosity so I dialed the number. A man answered with a cheery, "Hello! Church of God Grill!" I asked how his restaurant had been given such

an unusual name, and he told me: "Well, we had a little mission down here, and we started selling chicken dinners after church on Sunday to help pay the bills. Well, people liked the chicken, and we did such a good business, that eventually we cut back on the church stuff. After a while we just closed the door to the church altogether and kept on serving chicken dinners. We kept the name that we started with, and that's the Church of God Grill." [21]

I am committed that Stonebriar Community Church will not someday become Stonebriar Community Grill. I pray the same is true of your church—or of the one you're considering becoming a part of. *Grace . . . mentoring . . . fellowship . . . endurance.* If our churches added these characteristics to the essentials of Acts 2:42, we couldn't contain the crowds. Our churches would be incredibly unique, amazingly attractive. In a word, *contagious.*

It's one thing to agree that a church needs to have these qualities. But, if we've got them, how do we sustain them? How do we maintain our focus while living in a consumerist, postmodern culture? Here's the answer: *we must remember these distinctives and resist any sign of erosion.* Easy to say . . . but challenging to do. We must commit as a local church that we're not going to drift from the essentials of Acts 2:42 or from the characteristics of a contagious church.

If we drift, we change our whole identity. And when that happens we look and sound just like any other office building in town.

* * *

In our marketing-driven culture, many churches struggle with staying on task. A desire for church growth often overrides a commitment to biblical principles. How tragic . . . and unnecessary. A growing, contagious church includes each part of the body functioning as a healthy, caring, growing, and maturing whole. It's all about context. But as important as it is, even being a contagious church is not the *primary* purpose for the body to gather together on Sunday mornings. It's still something else.

That mound of stone Paul once stood on named Mars Hill was not the church. Paul's message to the intellectuals in Athens was never intended to be a model for our worship services. It *is*, however, a great example for personal *evangelism*. Does evangelism occur in the church? Absolutely! I can't remember a single Sunday morning service when I haven't shared the gospel message in some way. But evangelism isn't the *primary* purpose for believers to assemble on the Lord's Day. The reason isn't even "teaching them to obey"—though that, too, occurs. The Great Commission is the purpose of the universal church, lived out in the *daily* lives of the local church members. The essentials of Acts 2:42—*teaching, fellowship, breaking of bread*, and *prayer*—are the means through which Christian assemblies pursue this primary purpose on Sundays. They are what make for a healthy church body whose delight in the Lord is contagious!

So how is your church doing? Does it fulfill its purpose by focusing on these essentials? In my almost fifty years in ministry, I have never been more passionate, or hopeful, for church renewal. I believe the church can wake up, see how far it has drifted from its foundation, begin walking with God, and engage the culture for Jesus Christ. I pray that God will use this booklet in a powerful way to help *you* contribute to the structure Jesus is building. He promised: "I will build My church; and the gates of Hades will not overpower it" (Matthew 16:18).

How to Begin a Relationship with God

In an effort to reach our culture, many churches have wandered from their dependence on biblical truth. As a result, some congregations have devolved from communities of the gospel to centers of consumer-oriented entertainment, and some pastors have replaced God's nourishing Word with junk food. Often churches in a postmodern culture don't proclaim the gospel—and they don't explain the central role it should play in all of our lives.

So what is the gospel? The Bible explains the good news with four essential truths. Let's look at each truth in detail.

Our Spiritual Condition: Totally Depraved

The first truth is rather personal. One look in the mirror of Scripture, and our human condition becomes painfully clear:

"There is none righteous, not
    even one;
There is none who understands,
There is none who seeks for
    God;
All have turned aside, together
    they have become useless;
There is none who does good,
There is not even one."
    (Romans 3:10–12)

We are all sinners through and through—totally depraved. Now, that doesn't mean we've committed every atrocity known to humankind. We're not as *bad* as we can be, just as *bad off* as we can be. Sin colors all our thoughts, motives, words, and actions.

If you've been around a while, you likely already believe it. Look around. Everything around us bears the smudge marks of our sinful nature. Despite our best efforts to create a perfect world, crime statistics continue to soar, divorce rates keep climbing, and families keep crumbling.

Something has gone terribly wrong in our society and in ourselves—something deadly. Contrary to how the world would repackage it, "me-first" living doesn't equal rugged individuality and freedom; it equals death. As Paul said in his letter to the Romans, "The wages of sin is death" (Romans 6:23)—our spiritual and physical death that comes from God's righteous judgment of our sin, along with all of the emotional and practical effects of this separation that we experience on a daily basis. This brings us to the second marker: God's character.

God's Character: Infinitely Holy

How can God judge us for a sinful state we were born into? Our total depravity is only half the answer. The other half is God's infinite holiness.

The fact that we know things are not as they should be points us to a standard of goodness beyond ourselves. Our sense of injustice in life on this side of eternity implies a perfect standard of justice beyond our reality. That standard and source is God Himself. And God's standard of holiness contrasts starkly with our sinful condition.

Scripture says that "God is Light, and in Him there is no darkness at all" (1 John 1:5). God is absolutely holy—which creates a problem for us. If He is so pure, how can we who are so impure relate to Him?

Perhaps we could try being better people, try to tilt the balance in favor of our good deeds, or seek out methods for self-improvement. Throughout history, people have attempted to live up to God's standard by keeping the Ten Commandments or living by their own code of ethics. Unfortunately, no one can come close to satisfying the demands of God's law. Romans 3:20 says, "By the works of the Law no flesh will be justified in His sight; for through the Law comes the knowledge of sin."

Our Need: A Substitute

So here we are, sinners by nature and sinners by choice, trying to pull ourselves up by our own bootstraps to attain a relationship with our holy Creator. But every time we try, we fall flat on our faces. We can't live a good enough life to make up for our sin, because God's standard isn't "good enough"—it's *perfection*. And we can't make amends for the offense our sin has created without dying for it.

Who can get us out of this mess?

If someone could live perfectly, honoring God's law, and would bear sin's death penalty for us—in our place—then we would be saved from our predicament. But is there such a person? Thankfully, yes!

Meet your substitute—*Jesus Christ*. He is the One who took death's place for you!

> [God] made [Jesus Christ] who knew no sin to be sin on our behalf, so that we might become the righteousness of God in Him. (2 Corinthians 5:21)

God's Provision: A Savior

God rescued us by sending His Son, Jesus, to die on the cross for our sins (1 John 4:9–10). Jesus was fully human and fully divine (John 1:1, 18), a truth that ensures His understanding of our weaknesses, His power to forgive, and His ability to bridge the gap between God and us (Romans 5:6–11). In short, we are "justified as a gift by His grace through the redemption which is in Christ Jesus" (Romans 3:24). Two words in this verse bear further explanation: *justified* and *redemption*.

Justification is God's act of mercy, in which He declares righteous the believing sinners while we are still in our sinning state. Justification doesn't mean that God *makes* us righteous, so that we never sin again, rather that He *declares* us righteous—much like a judge pardons a guilty criminal. Because Jesus took our sin upon Himself and suffered our judgment on the cross, God forgives our debt and proclaims us PARDONED.

Redemption is Christ's act of paying the complete price to release us from sin's bondage. God sent His Son to bear His wrath for all of our sins—past, present, and future (Romans 3:24–26; 2 Corinthians 5:21). In humble obedience, Christ willingly endured the shame of the cross for our sake (Mark 10:45; Romans 5:6–8; Philippians 2:8). Christ's death satisfied God's righteous demands. He no longer holds our sins against us, because His own Son paid the penalty for them. We are freed from the slave market of sin, never to be enslaved again!

Placing Your Faith in Christ

These four truths describe how God has provided a way to Himself through Jesus Christ. Because the price has been paid in full by God, we must respond to His free gift of eternal life in total faith and confidence in Him to save us. We must step forward into the relationship with God that He has prepared for us—not by doing good works or by being a good person, but by coming to Him just as we are and accepting His justification and redemption by faith.

For by grace you have been saved through faith; and that not of yourselves, it is the gift of God; not as a result of works, so that no one may boast. (Ephesians 2:8–9)

We accept God's gift of salvation simply by placing our faith in Christ alone for the forgiveness of our sins. Would you like to enter a relationship with your Creator by trusting in Christ as your Savior? If so, here's a simple prayer you can use to express your faith:

Dear God,

I know that my sin has put a barrier between You and me. Thank You for sending Your Son, Jesus, to die in my place. I trust in Jesus alone to forgive my sins, and I accept His gift of eternal life. I ask Jesus to be my personal Savior and the Lord of my life. Thank You. In Jesus's name, amen.

If you've prayed this prayer or one like it and you wish to find out more about knowing God and His plan for you in the Bible, contact us at Insight for Living Ministries. Our contact information is on the following pages.

We Are Here for You

If you desire to find out more about knowing God and His plan for you in the Bible, contact us. Insight for Living Ministries provides staff pastors who are available for free written correspondence or phone consultation. These seminary-trained and seasoned counselors have years of experience and are well-qualified guides for your spiritual journey.

Please feel welcome to contact your regional office by using the information below:

United States
Insight for Living
Biblical Counseling Department
Post Office Box 269000
Plano, Texas 75026-9000
USA
972-473-5097 (Monday through Friday, 8:00 a.m. – 5:00 p.m. central time)
www.insight.org/contactapastor

Canada
Insight for Living Canada
Biblical Counseling Department
PO Box 8 Stn A
Abbotsford BC V2T 6Z4
CANADA
1-800-663-7639
info@insightforliving.ca

Australia, New Zealand, and South Pacific
Insight for Living Australia
Pastoral Care
Post Office Box 443
Boronia, VIC 3155
AUSTRALIA
1300 467 444

United Kingdom and Europe
Insight for Living United Kingdom
Pastoral Care
PO Box 553
Dorking
RH4 9EU
UNITED KINGDOM
0800 787 9364
+44 (0)1306 640156
pastoralcare@insightforliving.org.uk

Endnotes

Adapted from Charles R. Swindoll, "The Church: Let's Start Here" and "Distinctives of a Contagious Church," in *The Church Awakening: An Urgent Call for Renewal* (New York: FaithWords, 2010), 14–18, 69–107. Used by permission.

1. Story taken from Gene Weingarten, "Pearls Before Breakfast," *Washington Post*, April 8, 2007, http://www.washingtonpost.com/wp-dyn/content/article/2007/04/04/AR2007040401721.html (accessed May 17, 2012).

2. *Merriam-Webster's Collegiate Dictionary*, 11th ed. (Springfield, Mass.: Merriam-Webster, 2007), see "contagion."

3. F. F. Bruce, *The Spreading Flame: The Rise and Progress of Christianity from Its First Beginnings to the Conversion of the English* (Eugene, Ore.: Wipf & Stock, 2004).

4. Marty Neumeier, *The Brand Gap: How to Bridge the Distance Between Business Strategy and Design* (Berkeley, Calif.: New Riders, 2006), 41.

5. Tyler Wigg-Stevenson, "Jesus Is Not a Brand: Why It Is Dangerous to Make Evangelism Another Form of Marketing," *Christianity Today* 53, no. 1 (January 2009).

6. Molly Worthen, "Who Would Jesus Smack Down?" *New York Times* magazine (January 11, 2009), 20.

7. Phyllis Tickle, *The Great Emergence: How Christianity Is Changing and Why* (Grand Rapids: Baker Books, 2008), 162.

8. David Wells, *The Courage to Be Protestant: Truthlovers, Marketers, and Emergents in the Postmodern World* (Grand Rapids: Eerdmans, 2008), 77–78.

9. Wells, *The Courage to Be Protestant*, 11, 37.

10. Quote taken from videos at: http://revealnow .com/story.asp?storyid=49 (accessed June 3, 2009).

11. Walter Bauer and others, eds., *A Greek-English Lexicon of the New Testament and Other Early Christian Literature*, 2nd rev. ed. (Chicago: University of Chicago Press, 1979), 623.

12. Howard G. Hendricks, *Standing Together: Impacting Your Generation* (Gresham, Ore.: Vision House, 1995), 98.

13. Collin Hansen, "The X Factor: What Have We Learned from the Rise, Decline, and Renewal of 'Gen-X' Ministries?" *Leadership Journal*, http:// www.christianitytoday.com/le/2009/summer/ thexfactor.html (accessed May 17, 2012).

14. *Merriam-Webster's Collegiate Dictionary*, see "mentor."

15. Dietrich Bonhoeffer, *Life Together*, trans. John W. Doberstein (San Francisco: Harper&Row, 1954), 110–11.

16. Johannes P. Louw and Eugene A. Nida, eds., *Greek-English Lexicon of the New Testament Based on Semantic Domains*, 2nd ed. (New York: United Bible Societies, 1988, 1989). Electronic text hypertexted and prepared by OakTree Software, Inc. Version 3.2.

17. Dietrich Bonhoeffer, *The Cost of Discipleship*, rev. ed. (New York: Collier Books, MacMillan, 1959), 99.

18. Warren W. Wiersbe, *On Being a Servant of God*, rev. ed. (Grand Rapids: Baker Books, 2007), 46.

19. John R. W. Stott, *Guard the Gospel: The Message of 2 Timothy* (Downers Grove, Ill.: InterVarsity, 1974), 57–58.

20. Louw and Nida, *Greek-English Lexicon*.

21. Charles Paul Conn, *Making It Happen: A Christian Looks at Money, Competition, and Success* (Grand Rapids: Revell, 1981), 95.

Ordering Information

If you would like to order additional copies of *A Healthy Body: Characteristics of a Contagious Church* or order other Insight for Living Ministries resources, please contact the office that serves you.

United States
Insight for Living
Post Office Box 269000
Plano, Texas 75026-9000
USA
1-800-772-8888 (Monday through Friday, 7:00 a.m.–7:00 p.m. central time)
www.insight.org
www.insightworld.org

Canada
Insight for Living Canada
PO Box 8 Stn A
Abbotsford BC V2T 6Z4
CANADA
1-800-663-7639
www.insightforliving.ca

Australia, New Zealand, and South Pacific
Insight for Living Australia
Post Office Box 443
Boronia, VIC 3155
AUSTRALIA
1300 467 444
www.insight.asn.au

United Kingdom and Europe
Insight for Living United Kingdom
PO Box 553
Dorking
RH4 9EU
UNITED KINGDOM
0800 787 9364
www.insightforliving.org.uk

Other International Locations
International constituents may contact the
U.S. office through our Web site
(www.insightworld.org), mail queries, or by
calling +1-972-473-5136.